You ready to embark on a journey that's as sweet as a glass of lemonade on a hot Alabama afternoon? Well, sis, you're in for a treat as we dive deep into "Bytes and Sips".

We're fixin' to explore how technology, especially AI, is shapin' our daily lives down here in the South. So grab your favorite notebook or fire up your digital document because we're about to pen down some diary entries that'll make your mind wonder.

We'll sip some lemonade and pour out our thoughts about how AI impacts our daily routines. What apps do we use to navigate this modern world, and how does AI spice up our social media? But remember to ponder the good and the not-so-good side of AI in your life. Like a good southern pecan pie, technology's has its sweetness and a few bitter nuts too.

Next up, we've got some breakfast bytes. You're gonna pick a movie or TV show with a diverse cast, and as you watch, pay attention to how those characters are portrayed. Are they breakin' stereotypes or just mixin' up a blender full of bias? Write it down, and let's have a conversation about it.

Then, we're cracking the code. You'll put on detective hats. Research an AI algorithm, like those recommendation algorithms or facial recognition, and spill the beans about how they work and the impact they might be havin' on our society.

Next, we're gettin' real. Grab your journal and start jotin' down any microaggressions you experience or witness throughout the week. It could be as subtle as a whisper of magnolia in the breeze, but write it down, and let's chat about how these moments make you feel. Don't hold back, sis. We're here to listen.

s the journey continues, you become an AI outlaw. Here, it's all about creativity. Create an inventor character and imagine how this quirky character could help your journey to confront AI bias. Share your character's profile with someone close and see what they think.

ow, it's time to find an AI bias issue close to your heart and figure out ow you can get involved. Whether it's lending a helping hand, spreadin' awareness, or raisin' your voice, you're about to be a change-maker!

ter all the hard work, you take a break and sit down with your journal. Reflect on all you've learned on this journey and make a plan for what comes next.

entually, you craft your own personal manifesto, a battle cry to fight AI ias. You define your values, set your goals, and let your intentions be own to friends and family. You know it takes a community, and you're all in this together.

nally, you're gonna spread your wings beyond the South and learn how bias affects our global neighbors. Share your findings, and let's educate the world, one byte at a time.

So, my dear sis, let's gather 'round and dive deep into this guide. It's a roadmap for change, a taste of lemonade, and a dose of Southern hospitality all in one.

Get ready to unmask AI, one page at a time, and take control of your destiny!

Lemonade and Tech Talk:

Digital Diary

Digital Diary

Create a digital diary entry describing how technology, especially AI, shapes your daily life. What apps do you use?

Reflect on two positive and two negative aspects of AI in your life.

How does AI impact your social media experience or daily routines?

Breakfast Bytes:

Analyzing Diversity in Media

Diversity in Media

Pick a movie or TV show to watch with a diverse cast.

While watching, jot down the names of characters and note whether they break stereotypes or reinforce them.

Write a short review or reflection on how diversity is portrayed in the media you chose.

N O T E S

Cracking the Code:

Exploring the AI Algorithm

Exploring the AI Algorithms

Research an AI algorithm. (Ex. facial recognition)

Write a brief summary of how the algorithm works and its potential impact on society.

Reflect on the algorithm's potential for bias and how it reinforces stereotypes.

NOTES

Sips of Microaggressions:

Recognizing Micraggressions

Recognizing Micraggressions

Keep a journal for a week.

Record any incidents of microaggressions you experience or witness. These could be subtle comments, actions, or behaviors that make you feel uncomfortable or singled out.

How do these microaggressions affect you emotionally?

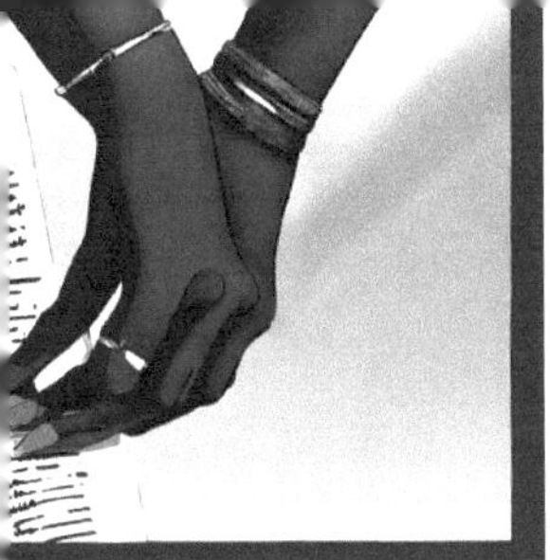

AI Outlaw :

Inventor Mind Map

Inventor Mind Map

Create a mind map or visual representation of a quirky inventor character, complete with their personality traits, appearance, and inventions.

Imagine how this character can aid in confronting AI bias.

Share your character profile with a friend or family member and get their input.

Empowerment:

Game Changers

Advocacy Plan

Identify an issue related to AI bias that you're passionate about.

Research local organizations or groups working on this issue.

Write down a plan on how you can get involved.

Ex. volunteering, organizing an awareness event, or starting a social media campaign.

NOTES

Sippin the Tea:

AI Knowledge

Sippin on the AI Knowledge

Take some time to reflect on your personal growth throughout this guide's journey.

Write a journal entry about what you've learned and how your perspective has evolved.

Identify any actions you plan to take to address AI bias in your life.

NOTES

Black Girl Manifesto:

Taking Control

Create a Personal Manifesto

Craft a personal manifesto outlining your commitment to combatting AI bias.

Define :

Your values
Goals
Actions you'll take

Share your manifesto with friends or family to inspire them to take action as well.

NOTES

Global Vibes:

Better Together

Researching the Global Impact

Research how AI bias affects marginalized communities in different parts of the world.

Create a short presentation summarizing your findings.

Share your research with friends or classmates to raise awareness about global AI bias issues.

REMEMBER, THESE ACTIVITIES ARE DESIGNED TO ENGAGE, EDUCATE, AND EMPOWER YOU IN THE FIGHT AGAINST AI BIAS.

THEY'LL HELP YOU TAKE REAL STEPS TOWARD POSITIVE CHANGE WHILE HAVING FUN ALONG THE WAY!